Flicking
the Switch

by Brian Birchall
illustrated by Donna Cross

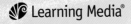
Learning Media®

Contents

1, Jack Peterson

Can you imagine what life would be like without electricity? Think of all the times that you switch something on each day. How would you get by if there were no electric lights, refrigerators, or televisions?

A hundred and fifty years ago, there was no electricity. People's lives were very different, and they worked very hard, but they still had fun.

This is Jack Peterson. Jack was born in 1851. There was no electricity when he was growing up.

Let's see how Jack and his family lived – without electricity.

2. In the Oven

Jack's family cooked on an iron **stove**. They were lucky. Some of their neighbors had to cook over a **fireplace**.

Jack liked to have a hot drink with his breakfast. This is what he had to do to heat the water for his drink:

1. Chop some firewood for **kindling**.
2. Set and light a fire in the stove.
3. Put a kettle of cold water on the stove.
4. Keep the fire burning until the water was hot.

Sometimes the wood was damp. Then the stove could take more than thirty minutes to heat up.

Jack's family usually lit the fire early in the morning and kept it going all day.

Today, you could make a hot drink and toast as well – all before Jack could have gotten the fire started!

Did you know ...

that each burner on an electric stove has a heating wire inside it. The electricity flows through the wire and heats the burner. When you put a pan on top, the pan heats up, too.

3. Light at Night

When Jack wanted to see at night, he had only firelight, a candle, or an **oil lamp**. The light from firelight and candles was very weak. Oil lamps gave a better light, but the burning oil was smelly. The lamps had to be refilled every day.

Lamplight was still too weak for reading or writing. Sometimes Jack and his family would sing or tell stories after supper. Usually they went to bed early.

Jack kept a candle beside his bed, just in case he needed to get up in the middle of the night.

Now, you can read, write, or play all day *and* all night! You don't have to stop when the sun goes down. And if you need to get up in the middle of the night, you just flick a switch. It's almost as light as day!

Did you know ...

that a light bulb has a thin **coil** of wire inside it. When you flick on a light switch, electricity goes through the wire. The wire gets hot. It gets so hot that it glows white. This is how light is made from electricity.

4. Warming Up

Jack and his family worked hard all year to make sure that they would be warm in winter.

In summer, Jack's father cut down trees from the forest.

In fall, he sawed the trees into logs. Jack and his brothers and sisters stacked the logs in the barn.

In winter, they cut up the dry logs to use in the stove and the fireplace. Every day, they carried firewood into the house. It was very heavy work.

Jack's family only heated the main room of their house, to save firewood. The rest of the house was freezing in winter.

Jack put on extra clothes if he felt cold. Everyone had big, heavy **quilts** on their beds. Sometimes the children slept together in one bed to keep warm.

Jack's cousins lived in the city. They used **coal** instead of firewood in their stove and fireplace. His cousins carried the coal in buckets. The buckets were very heavy!

Today, we use electricity to keep our houses warm. We just flick a switch to turn on an electric heater. Many buildings and houses have **central heating**, which warms every room.

Electricity heats water for us, too. We can warm up in the bathtub if we're really cold!

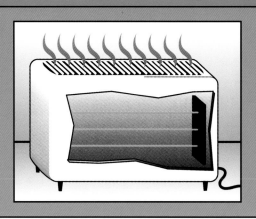

Did you know ...

that there are heating wires inside an electric heater. When electricity goes through the wires, it makes them hot. The hot wires make the air hot.

Some heaters also have fans inside them. The fans push the hot air out into the room.

5, Big News

Jack had some news to tell his cousins in the city. He wrote a letter to them. Then he asked someone to take it to the post office in the nearest town.

Jack's letter had to travel to the city on the **stagecoach**.

Travel was slow and dangerous in those days. A letter could take weeks to arrive. If the stagecoach had an accident, Jack's letter might not get there at all. Then it could take just as long for a letter from Jack's cousins to get back. By that time, the news was pretty old!

Today, we can share our news the day it happens. We can use the telephone or fax, or we can use email. These all use electricity. We can send our news to people on the other side of the world in a flash.

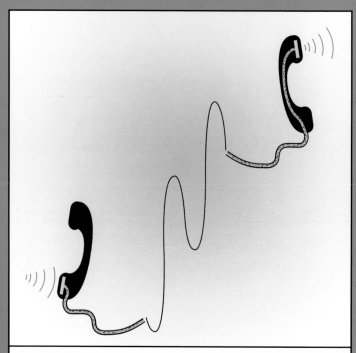

Did you know ...

that inside the telephone, your voice is changed into thousands of electrical signals. The signals travel through the phone wires. When they get to the phone at the other end, they change back into your voice.

6. Power for Fun

Jack didn't have a TV when he was a boy. Television hadn't even been invented! He liked to watch shows and plays, though.

Sometimes a show would travel around, and Jack and his family would go to see it when it came near their home.

One day, a circus came to a town close to Jack's home. His family walked into town to see it. It was a long way, but they didn't mind. It was such a special event.

The circus was held during the day because lamplight was not bright enough to have shows at night.

Now, we have TV, video, and the Internet. You can see all kinds of shows any day or night without leaving your home.

You might think that life would be dull without these things. But Jack and his family had no time to be bored. They were too busy playing together and helping with chores.

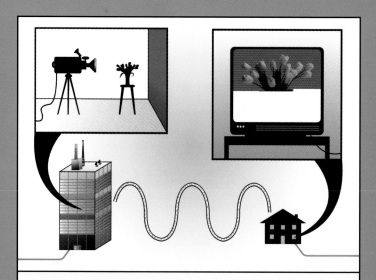

that electricity is used to transport pictures from the TV station to your TV set. The picture is broken up into thousands of tiny dots called pixels. The pixels travel through wires or radio waves. When they get to your TV, they move back into place in the picture.

7. A Visit from Jack

How do you think Jack would feel if he could see you in your home? Imagine if he could see you watching TV or listening to your stereo!

Jack would be amazed by all the things that you can do just by pressing a button or flicking a switch. He might want to flick every switch in your house!

Glossary

(These words are printed in bold type the first time they appear in the book.)

central heating: a system that heats a whole building

coal: a black rock that can be burned

coil: a shape that curls around and around

fireplace: a place with a chimney for making a fire in a house

kindling: small sticks of firewood used to start a fire

oil lamp: a small light that burns oil

quilt: a cover for a bed, usually filled with feathers

stagecoach: a horse-drawn coach used for long-distance travel

stove: something that is used to heat a building or to cook food

Index